DIGGING UP THE PAST

ANCIENT FOOTPRINTS

BY TRUDY BECKER

WWW.APEXEDITIONS.COM

Copyright © 2026 by Apex Editions, Mendota Heights, MN 55120. All rights reserved. No part of this book may be reproduced or utilized in any form or by any means without written permission from the publisher.

Apex is distributed by North Star Editions:
sales@northstareditions.com | 888-417-0195

Produced for Apex by Red Line Editorial.

Photographs ©: iStockphoto, cover, 4–5; Nick Ashton, Simon G. Lewis, Isabelle De Groote, et al./PLOS One, 6–7; Shutterstock Images, 1, 9, 10–11, 12, 13, 16–17, 20, 22–23; Fidelis T. Masao, Elgidius B. Ichumbaki, Marco Cherin, et al./eLife, 14, 18; USGS, 19; NPS, 24, 25, 29; Gongga Laisong/China News Service/Getty Images, 26–27

Library of Congress Control Number: 2024952838

ISBN
979-8-89250-529-1 (hardcover)
979-8-89250-565-9 (paperback)
979-8-89250-635-9 (ebook pdf)
979-8-89250-601-4 (hosted ebook)

Printed in the United States of America
Mankato, MN
082025

NOTE TO PARENTS AND EDUCATORS

Apex books are designed to build literacy skills in striving readers. Exciting, high-interest content attracts and holds readers' attention. The text is carefully leveled to allow students to achieve success quickly. Additional features, such as bolded glossary words for difficult terms, help build comprehension.

TABLE OF CONTENTS

CHAPTER 1
BEACH STORM 4

CHAPTER 2
FINDING FOOTPRINTS 10

CHAPTER 3
TOOLS AND TECHNOLOGY 16

CHAPTER 4
LOTS TO LEARN 22

COMPREHENSION QUESTIONS • 28
GLOSSARY • 30
TO LEARN MORE • 31
ABOUT THE AUTHOR • 31
INDEX • 32

CHAPTER 1

BEACH STORM

In 2013, a storm rages in Happisburgh, England. Waves crash onto the shore. They wash away sand and **sediment**. They reveal many markings.

Happisburgh sits on the east coast of England.

After the storm, a team of scientists go to the shore. They see the markings in the rocky ground. The storm has uncovered ancient footprints.

The Happisburgh footprints came from a small group of adults and children.

The scientists record their findings. They start to **excavate** more prints. But the team must act fast. In just weeks, waves will wash the prints away.

CHANGING LAND

Today, Happisburgh is close to the sea. Thousands of years ago, the land looked different. The town was farther from the sea. The ground near the shore was soft and wet. People left footprints in it.

Waves wear away the coast of Happisburgh. The cliffs lose nearly 10 feet (3 m) of land each year.

CHAPTER 2

FINDING FOOTPRINTS

Archaeologists often examine objects such as bones and tools. But they study **trace fossils**, too. Those include footprints from the past.

Archaeologists search for bones and items left by people who lived long ago.

In the 1800s, researchers went to Lake Onega in Russia. They found carvings and footprints in the ground.

Most footprints vanish over time. But some get covered by new material. The buried prints are preserved. Later, **erosion** may uncover them.

WALKING BY WATER

Most ancient footprints are near water. In 2022, scientists found prints on a Morocco beach. A family left them 100,000 years ago. They were heading to the water.

Land near water is soft. But it may harden into rock.

In the 1970s, a team found footprints at Laetoli in Tanzania. The prints were saved in volcanic ash. They came from an early human **species**.

FAST FACT
The Laetoli footprints are 3.6 million years old.

◀ The footprints at Laetoli form a trail. It includes about 70 prints made by early humans.

CHAPTER 3

Tools and Technology

Footprint sites are delicate. Scientists need to be careful. They may use soft brushes to move soil.

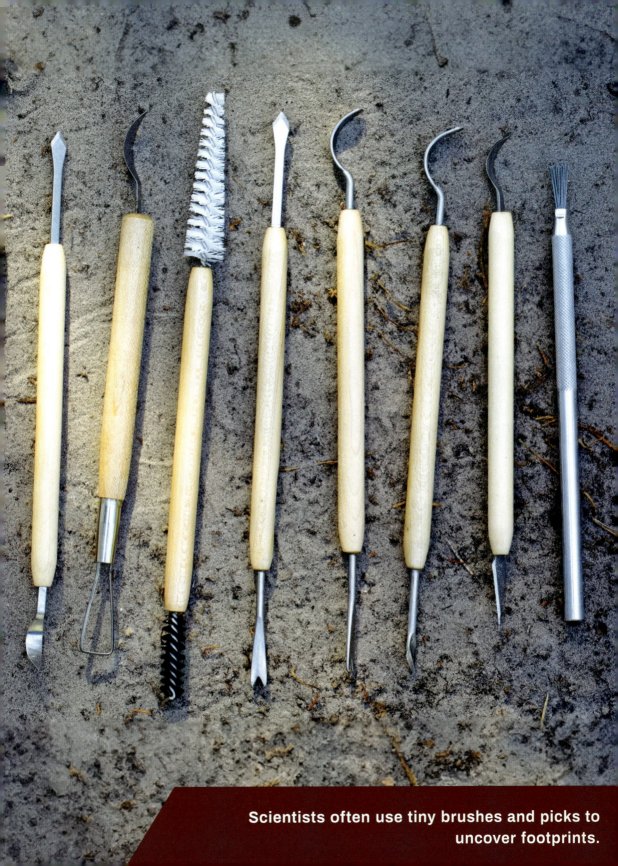

Scientists often use tiny brushes and picks to uncover footprints.

The spacing between footprints can show people's heights. Short people leave closely spaced footprints.

Scientists take pictures of footprints from all angles. Then, computers make 3D models. People can learn the heights and weights of the ancient humans. They can learn their ages, too.

FAST FACT
Scientists sometimes use **drones** to study prints. The drones take pictures from above.

Drones help scientists view prints from a distance.

19

Other technology dates the footprints. Scientists look at the rock around the prints. They study its layers. They may also use **carbon dating**. Both help show how old the prints are.

LOTS OF LAYERS

Layers of rock and soil build up over time. Newer layers are added at the top. However, layers sometimes shift. This can make dating tricky.

◀ Rock formed from sediment has many layers. Some layers are different colors.

CHAPTER 4

LOTS TO LEARN

Ancient footprints teach scientists about past humans. Prints can show where people searched for food. They can show whether people traveled in groups.

Archaeologists try to learn how ancient people lived, hunted, and even played.

In 2009, scientists found 61 footprints at White Sands. In 2018, they found even more prints.

Some footprints change ideas. Historians once thought humans came to North America about 15,000 years ago. Then, people found footprints at White Sands in New Mexico. The prints were around 21,000 years old.

HUMANS AND ANIMALS

Scientists learn from animal prints, too. The White Sands area has giant sloth prints. Human footprints follow them closely. So, scientists think humans likely hunted sloths.

Scientists found a human footprint in a giant sloth print. Giant sloths weighed thousands of pounds.

In 2018, scientists found handprints and footprints in China. The prints appeared to be artwork made by children about 200,000 years ago.

In 2024, people were still learning more from White Sands. And they were finding more prints around the world. Scientists still had lots to discover about the past.

FAST FACT

People have found ancient footprints on every continent except Antarctica.

COMPREHENSION QUESTIONS

Write your answers on a separate piece of paper.

1. Write a few sentences describing the main idea of Chapter 3.

2. Would you like to work as an archaeologist? Why or why not?

3. How old were the footprints in Happisburgh?
   - A. 100,000 years old
   - B. 900,000 years old
   - C. 3.6 million years old

4. Why do scientists photograph ancient footprints?
   - A. so the footprints will last longer
   - B. so they can study the prints in new ways and places
   - C. so other people cannot see or study the footprints

5. What does **examine** mean in this book?

*Archaeologists often **examine** objects such as bones and tools. But they study trace fossils, too.*

   A. throw away
   B. look closely at
   C. ignore

6. What does **delicate** mean in this book?

*Footprint sites are **delicate**. Scientists need to be careful. They may use soft brushes to move soil.*

   A. strong and rough
   B. cold and icy
   C. easy to break

Answer key on page 32.

GLOSSARY

archaeologists
People who study long-ago times, often by digging up things from the past.

carbon dating
Calculating the age of something based on the amount of a certain carbon in it.

drones
Aircraft that people control from far away.

erosion
When something slowly wears away over time.

excavate
To dig up or uncover something.

sediment
Stone, sand, or other material carried by wind, water, or ice.

species
A group of animals or plants that are similar and can breed with one another.

trace fossils
Paths or signs left by ancient life.

TO LEARN MORE

BOOKS

Neuenfeldt, Elizabeth. *Giant Ground Sloths*. Bellwether Media, 2025.

Owen, Ruth. *Rocks: Let's Investigate*. Ruby Tuesday Books, 2021.

Petersen, Christine. *Unearth Fossils*. Abdo Publishing, 2020.

ONLINE RESOURCES

Visit **www.apexeditions.com** to find links and resources related to this title.

ABOUT THE AUTHOR

Trudy Becker lives in Minneapolis, Minnesota. She likes exploring new places and loves anything involving books.

INDEX

A
Antarctica, 27
archaeologists, 10

C
carbon dating, 21

D
drones, 19

E
erosion, 12

H
Happisburgh, England, 4, 7–8

L
Laetoli, Tanzania, 15

M
Morocco, 13

S
sediment, 4
species, 15

T
trace fossils, 10

W
White Sands, New Mexico, 24–25, 27

ANSWER KEY:
1. Answers will vary; 2. Answers will vary; 3. B; 4. B; 5. B; 6. C